Bond Assessment Papers

Starter papers in Reasoning

J M Bond

Paper 1

1–5 Write these words in the correct group. 2

girl cat man lad cow

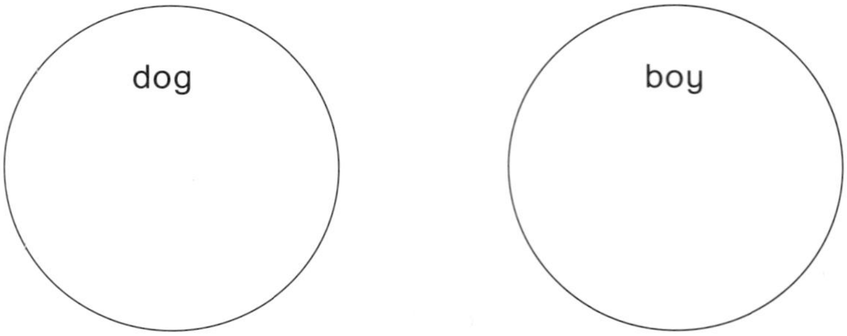

5

Underline the pair of shapes that are most similar.

6

7

2

Change the first word into the last word by changing one letter at a time. 26
The word in the middle must be a real word.

Example ON → AN → AT

8 IS ______ OF

9 UP ______ IS

10 BE ______ MY

11 AS ______ IF

12 HE ______ BY

5

Underline one word from the brackets so that the sentences make sense. 33

Example The (car, <u>cow</u>, table) was eating grass.

13 They sat down on a (lamp, seat, wave).

14 She cooked some (ice-cream, rice, car).

15 The cat ate its (wood, dish, food).

16 He put the book on the (table, oven, water).

17 The stars were in the (dress, sky, box). 5

If ACC is the code for BEE 45

18 CAA is the code for ____________.

If ABC is the code for SET

19 ABB is the code for ____________.

If GHJ is the code for WET

20 GHH is the code for ____________. 3

The ages of 3 boys total 20 years. A is 6 and B is a year older than A. 47

21 How old is B? ____________ 22 How old is C? ____________ 2

A B C D E F G H I J K L M N O P Q R S T U V W X Y Z

23 Make a word from the 5th, 7th and 7th letters of the alphabet.

____

24 Make a word from the 2nd, 1st and 4th letters of the alphabet.

____

25 Make a word from the 4th, 5th, 1st and 6th letters of the alphabet.

____________ 3

25 TOTAL

Paper 2

Underline the pair of words most similar in meaning. 3

Example laugh, cry dog, cat <u>say, speak</u>

1 quick, fast cold, hot up, down

2 good, bad dress, girl boy, lad

3 fish, shoe cat, kitten walk, sleep

4 bun, plate pen, fork dog, puppy

5 chair, seat meat, spoon tea, sit 5

Underline the shape in the brackets most similar to the shape outside the brackets.

6

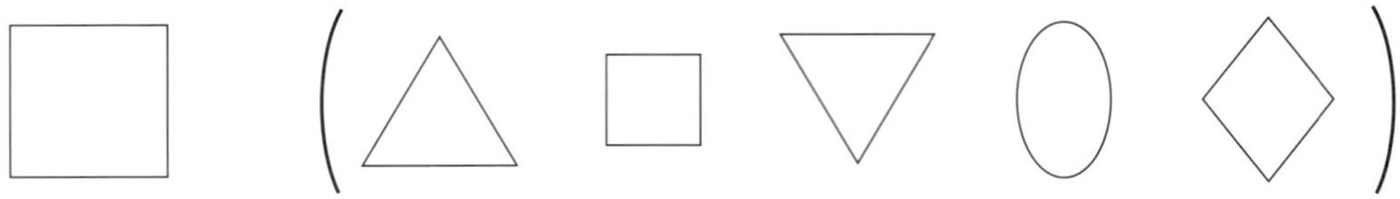

7

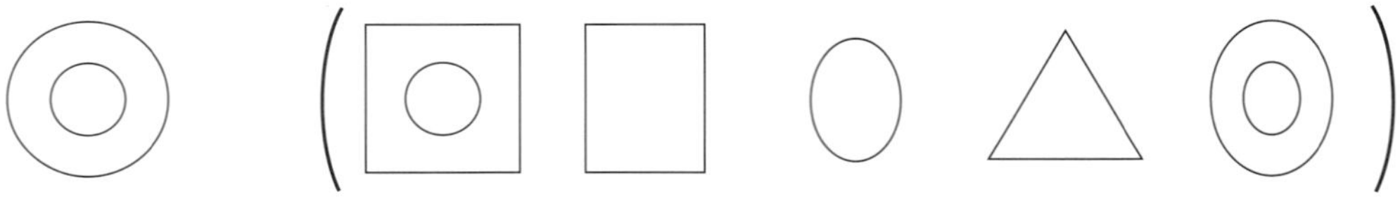

2

Change the first word of the third pair in the same way as the other pairs. 27

Example DIG → DOG
FIG → FOG
BIG → *BOG*

8 WET → WIT
SET → SIT
PET → ________

9 NET → NUT
PET → PUT
BET → ________

10 LIT → LET
BIT → BET
WIT → ________

11 GET → GOT
LET → LOT
NET → ________

12 CAN → CAT
FAN → FAT
BAN → ________

5

Write these words in alphabetical order. 43

Example TRUCK CAR BUS VAN *BUS CAR TRUCK VAN*

13 CAP PAT HAT

(1) ________ (2) ________ (3) ________

14 PIN TIN BIN

(1) ________ (2) ________ (3) ________

15 LET MET JET

(1) ________ (2) ________ (3) ________

16 FED BED WED

(1) ________ (2) ________ (3) ________ 4

If TWO is written in code as ABC 45

17 TOO is written in code as ________.

If FED is written in code as CXY

18 FEE is written in code as ________.

If AND is written in code as RSP

19 ADD is written in code as ________. 3

A has 8p and B has twice as much as A. 47

20 B has ________. **21** Together they have ________. 2

Circle the correct answer each time.

22 I buy an ice-cream for 90p. How much will I have left from a £1 coin? 50

20p 10p 5p 15p

23 I buy 2 lots of sweets, each costing 40p. How much will I have left from a £1 coin?

2p 10p 20p 40p

24 Together we had 12 sweets. A had 4, B had 3 and I had the rest. How many did I have?

5 4 3 2

In a test A gets 9 marks and B gets 6 marks.

25 How many more marks did A have than B?

2 3 4 5

4

25 TOTAL

Paper 3

Underline the word in the brackets closest in meaning to the word in capitals. 4

Example SAD (happy, unhappy, friendly)

1 SHOE (leg, boot, jumper)

2 CUP (drink, plate, mug)

3 RUSH (hurry, slow, walk)

4 NEW (old, fresh, dirty)

5 RING (square, oblong, circle) 5

Underline the two shapes, one from each group, that are most similar.

6

7

2

Add a letter to the front of the capital letters so that the sentences make sense. 30

Example Grass is GREEN.

8 I hurt my ____EG playing football.

9 My friend has long blond ____AIR.

10 You wear gloves to keep your ____ANDS warm.

11 I liked reading my ____OOK.

12 I'm going to ____RITE a thank you note. 5

Fill in the missing letter in each sequence. The alphabet has been written out to help you. 35

A B C D E F G H I J K L M N O P Q R S T U V W X Y Z

Example A is to B as C is to D

13 A is to B as D is to ____

14 A is to D as B is to ____

15 B is to C as G is to ____

16 D is to F as C is to ____

17 G is to I as H is to ____ 5

Write these words in alphabetical order. 43

Example TRUCK CAR BUS VAN BUS CAR TRUCK VAN

18 DAY WAY SAY

(1) ________ (2) ________ (3) ________

19 HIT SIT BIT

(1) ________ (2) ________ (3) ________

20 WET SET GET

(1) ________ (2) ________ (3) ________

21 JOY TOY BOY

(1) ________ (2) ________ (3) ________ 4

B has 12p and C has 3p more than B. 47

22 C has ________. **23** Together they have ________. 2

A train takes 1 hour to travel from Laptown to London.

24–25 Fill in the missing times.

LAPTOWN (depart)	LONDON (arrive)
________	11.00
14.00	________

2

25 TOTAL

Paper 4

1–3 Write the letter of each shape in the correct group.

a) 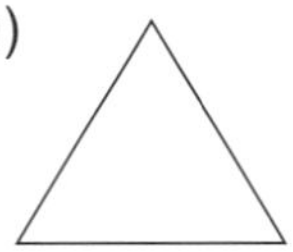

b) 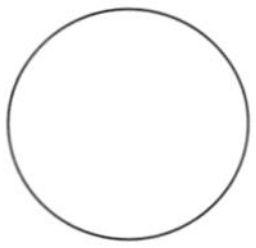

c) 

No corners **Corners**

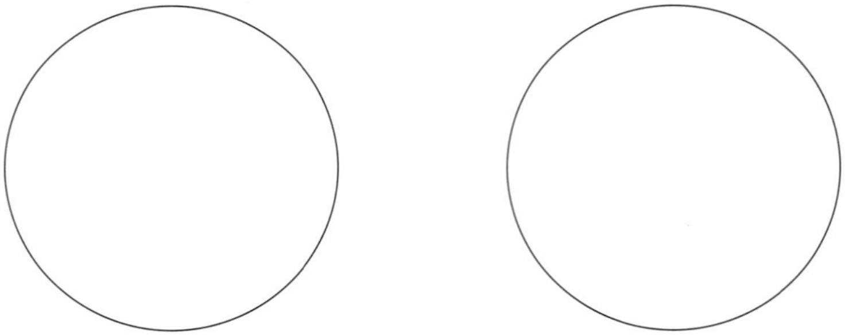

3

Underline the two words, one from each group, which are closest in meaning. 5

Example (<u>shut</u>, open) (<u>close</u>, window)

4 (begin, work) (paper, start)

5 (big, tower) (large, man)

6 (rain, hot) (drizzle, cold)

7 (tea, cake) (hungry, bun)

8 (dry, damp) (wet, cold) 5

Remove one letter from the word in capital letters to leave a new word. The meaning of the new word is given in the clue. 31

Example OPEN something you write with PEN

9 COST a baby's bed ________

10 TALL everyone ________

11 BLOW the opposite of 'high' ________

12 ROAD a kind of stick ________

13 FROG a mist ________ 5

Underline one word from the brackets so that the sentences make sense. 33

Example The (car, cow, table) was eating grass.

14 The snowman was (fighting, melting, talking).

15 Mum put our toys in the (box, jug, kettle).

16 We had (floor, flower, fish) for our supper.

17 She wore a (coat, cat, cow) as she was cold.

18 The car was in the (rug, garage, room). 5

Complete the following expressions by underlining the correct word in the brackets. 37

Example Boy is to girl as man is to (woman, grown-up, person).

19 Girl is to woman as boy is to (adult, man, lady).

20 Laugh is to happy as cry is to (sad, glad, fun).

21 Bird is to fly as fish is to (water, sky, swim).

22 Pig is to sty as man is to (house, barn, tree).

23 Cat is to kitten as dog is to (lead, puppy, collar). 5

A's watch is 2 minutes slow. Write what time her watch shows when it is: 47

24 12.10 ____________ **25** 13.05 ____________ 2

25 TOTAL

Paper 5

1–5 Write these words in the correct group. 2

run cry shout walk yell

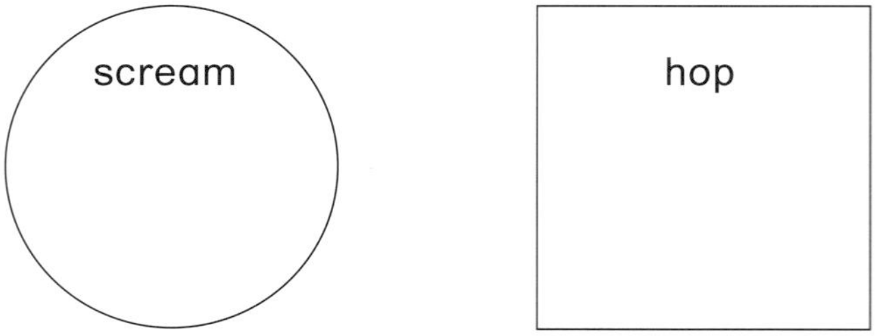

5

Change the first word into the last word by changing one letter at a time. The word in the middle must be a real word. 26

Example ON → AN → AT

6 US ____________ IT

7 AN ____________ IF

8 BY ____________ WE

9 MA ____________ BY

10 HE ____________ MY 5

Underline one shape in the brackets to complete the sequence.

11

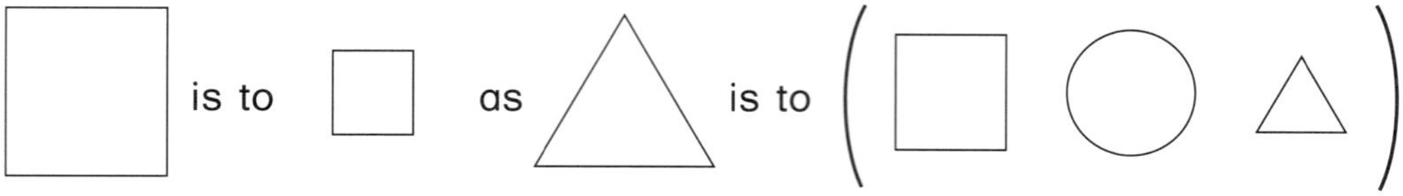

12

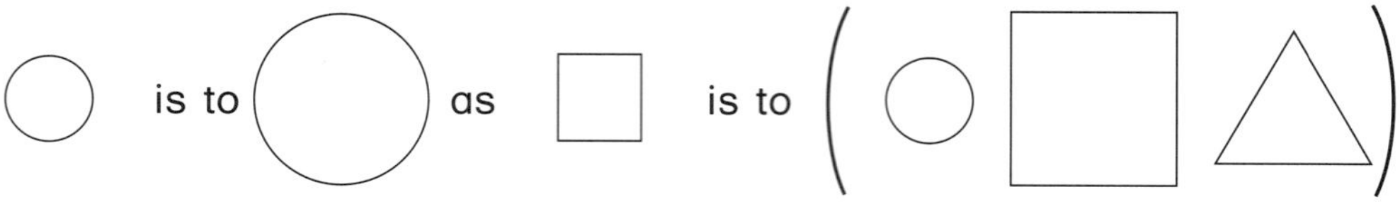

2

Write the missing number or numbers in each sequence. 42

Example 1 2 3 4 5

13 1 3 5 ____ 9

14 12 11 ____ 9 8

15–16 ____ 2 ____ 4 5 4

If DAD is written in code as 717 45

17 ADD is written in code as ________.

If CAT is written in code as 345

18 ACT is written in code as ________.

If TAP is written in code as 675

19 PAT is written in code as ________. 3

If a = 1 b = 2 c = 3 d = 4 what is the value of the following? 49

20 b + a + d = ________

21 c + a + b = ________

22 d + a + c = ________ 3

These are the number of children who were away from school during 1 week. 47

MONDAY	TUESDAY	WEDNESDAY	THURSDAY	FRIDAY
3	0	2	1	5

23 On which day were no children absent? ________

24 On which day were the most children absent? ________

25 On which day were 3 children absent? ________ 3

25 TOTAL

Paper 6

Underline the pair of words most similar in meaning. 3

Example laugh, cry dog, cat <u>say, speak</u>

1 farm, school cow, mad cot, bed

2 dog, cat mug, cup wet, dry

3 pen, pencil red, book walk, hot

4 late, shut start, begin early, go

5 game, out hush, go cry, shout 5

Underline the shape in the brackets most similar to the shape outside the brackets.

6 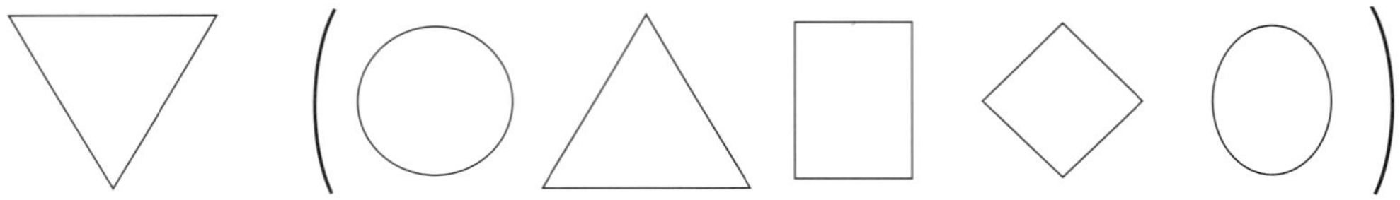

7 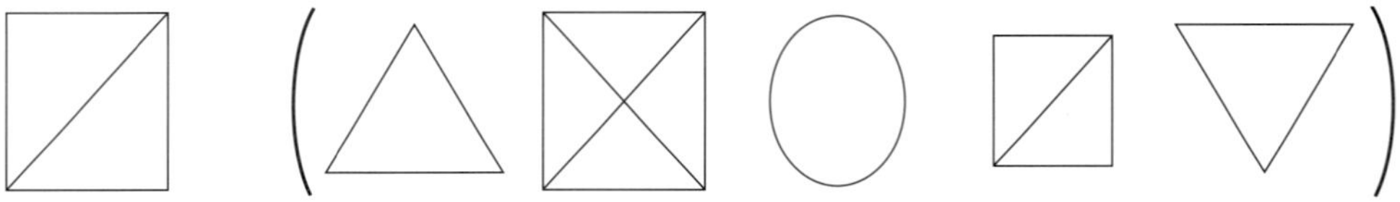

2

Rearrange the muddled letters to make a proper word so that the sentences make sense. 17

Example I can read a KOBO. BOOK

8 I went to DBE as I was tired. ______________

9 My little sister sleeps in a OCT. ______________

10 I took my OGD for a walk. ______________ 3

Underline the one word in each group which cannot be made from the letters in capitals. 19

Example ABCD bad cad <u>ace</u> dab

11 DREAD dad red and are

12 TABLE tea all bat let 2

Change the first word of the third pair in the same way as the other pairs. | 27

Example DIG → DOG
FIG → FOG
BIG → *BOG*

13 DAB → DUB
CAB → CUB
TAB → ______

14 SET → SAT
BET → BAT
MET → ______

15 FET → JOT
NET → NOT
PET → ______

16 BUG → BAG
TUG → TAG
LUG → ______

17 CAN → CAT
LOP → LAP
TOP → ______

5

Give the next group of letters in each sequence. | 41

Example A B C *D*

18 A AB AC ______

19 C CD CE ______

20 D DE DF ______

21 E EF EG ______

4

If 913 is the code for TAR | 45

22 139 is the code for ______.

If 234 is the code for POT

23 432 is the code for ______.

If 678 is the code for PAN

24 876 is the code for ______.

If 971 is the code for GET

25 799 is the code for ______.

4

25 TOTAL

Paper 7

Underline the word in the brackets closest in meaning to the word in capitals. 4

Example SAD (happy, <u>unhappy</u>, friendly)

1 HIGH (low, fat, tall)

2 PAINT (colour, tin, brush)

3 HUG (bag, cuddle, cut)

4 PAIR (shoes, four, two)

5 LOOK (see, picture, book) 5

Rearrange the muddled letters so that the sentences make sense. 18

Example My UMM *mum* drinks ETA *tea*.

6 The ANM __________ went for a walk with his ODG __________.

7 It AWS __________ raining and the ground was very ETW __________.

8 ADD __________ likes cakes for ETA __________. 3

Add a letter to the front of the capital letters so that the sentences make sense. 30

Example Grass is *G*REEN.

9 You have 10 ____OES on your feet.

10 You have a ____HUMB on each hand.

11 You breathe through your ____OSE.

12 You hear with your ____ARS.

13 Your ____LBOW is part of your arm. 5

Underline one word from the brackets so that the sentences make sense. 33

Example The (car, <u>cow</u>, table) was eating grass.

14 The (pony, lady, car) was reading a book.

15 The (bus, bud, cow) arrived late.

16 The (fox, train, driver) was in the car.

17 The (horse, boy, comb) was brushing his hair.

18 The (last, girl, lamp) was eating her supper. 5

Fill in the missing letter in each sequence. The alphabet has been written out to help you. 35

A B C D E F G H I J K L M N O P Q R S T U V W X Y Z

Example A is to B as C is to D

19 C is to F as D is to ____

20 C is to H as B is to ____

21 B is to E as C is to ____

22 A is to F as C is to ____

23 B is to F as D is to ____ 5

Draw the missing shape in each sequence.

24

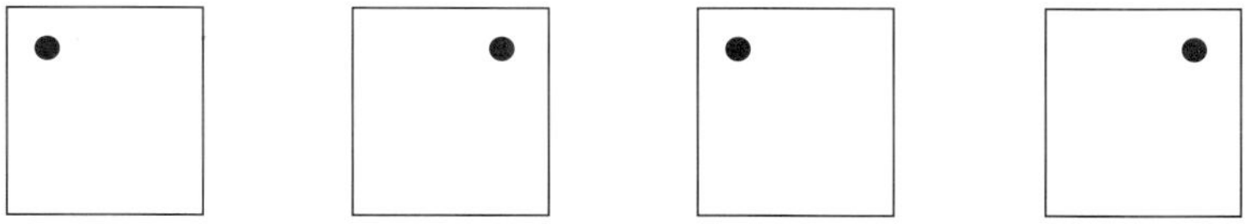

____

25

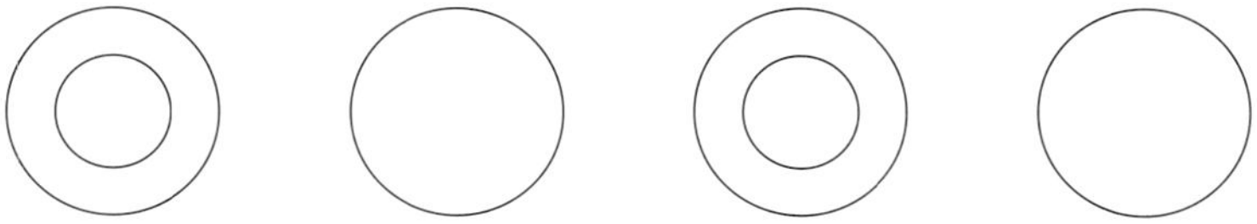

____ 2

25 TOTAL

Paper 8

Underline the pair of shapes that are most similar.

1

2

2

Underline the two words, one from each group, which are closest in meaning. 5

Example (shut, open) (close, window)

3 (door, close) (near, far)

4 (size, small) (short, big)

5 (jump, rope) (run, hop)

6 (floor, brush) (sweep, ceiling)

7 (begin, end) (finish, work) 5

Underline the two words which are made from the same letters. 22

Example two too tow wet ten

8 nip pen pun pin pan

9 kit ink ken nut kin

10 beg bug gas bag sag 3

Remove one letter from the word in capital letters to leave a new word. The meaning of the new word is given in the clue. 31

Example OPEN something you write with PEN

11 HOOP a jump on one foot ________

12 MATE a kind of rug ________

13 BOUT the opposite of 'in' ________

14 MICE frozen water ________

15 COLD not young ________ 5

Complete the following expressions by underlining the correct word or number in the brackets. 37

Example Boy is to girl as man is to (woman, grown-up, person).

16 Triangle is to 3 as square is to (2, 4, 3).

17 Drink is to water as eat is to (food, meal, supper).

18 Ant is to insect as lion is to (farm, animal, forest).

19 Night is to dark as day is to (light, morning, dawn).

20 Write is to pen as paint is to (paper, brush, pencil). 5

Write these words in alphabetical order. 43

Example TRUCK CAR BUS VAN BUS CAR TRUCK VAN

21 SUP MUG CUP

(1) ____________ (2) ____________ (3) ____________

22 FIG LOG BOG

(1) ____________ (2) ____________ (3) ____________

23 MEN HEN PEN

(1) ____________ (2) ____________ (3) ____________ 3

24–25 Each lesson lasts 30 minutes. Complete the table. 47

Lesson starts	Lesson ends
09.00	09.30
09.30	____________
10.00	____________

2

25 TOTAL

Paper 9

2

1–5 Write these words in the correct group.

coat pencil crayon hat pen

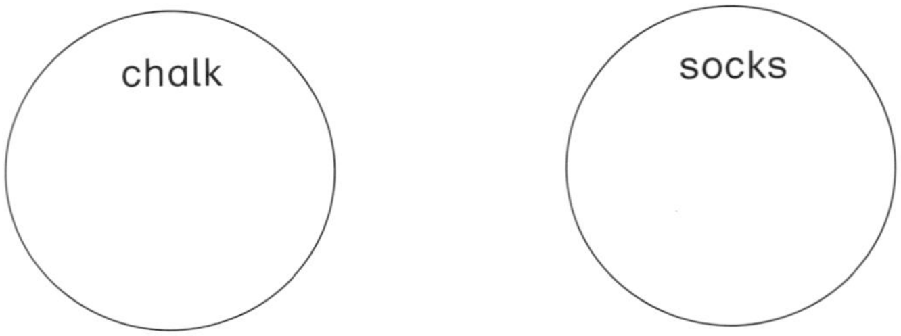

5

Underline the two shapes, one from each group, that are most similar.

6

7

2

Rearrange the muddled letters to make a proper word so that the sentences make sense. 17

Example I can read a KOBO. BOOK

8 The ACT sat on the rug. __________

9 The OWC gives us milk. __________

10 The plant was in a pretty OTP. __________

3

Change the first word into the last word by changing one letter at a time. The word in the middle must be a real word. 26

Example ON → AN → AT

11 UP __________ IS

12 OF __________ IT

13 WE ________ BY

14 US ________ AT

15 ME ________ BY

5

Write these words in alphabetical order.

43

Example TRUCK CAR BUS VAN BUS CAR TRUCK VAN

16 MAN CAN PAN

(1) ________ (2) ________ (3) ________

17 RED BED LED

(1) ________ (2) ________ (3) ________

18 HUT POT CUT

(1) ________ (2) ________ (3) ________

19 ANT EVE BEE

(1) ________ (2) ________ (3) ________

20 SEA ATE BUN

(1) ________ (2) ________ (3) ________

5

In a code BEAD is written as 2514

45

Write these words using the same code.

21 BAD ________ 22 BED ________ 23 ADD ________

3

I am having a party on Tuesday, December 20th. My friend is having her party 3 days after mine.

47

24 On what day and date is her party? ________________

We start school a week after my birthday, which is on September 2nd. Underline the date when we start school.

25 August 9th September 9th September 10th

2

25 TOTAL

Paper 10

1–2 Write the letter of each shape in the correct group.

a) 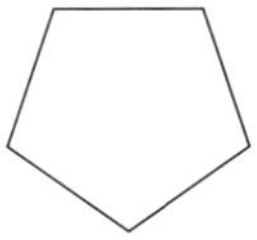

b) 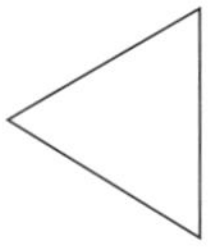

Fewer than 4 corners

More than 4 corners

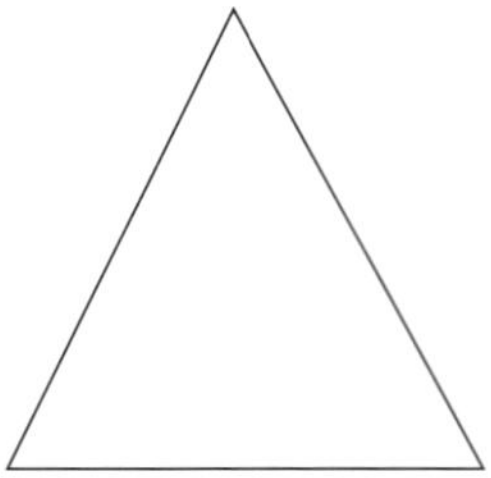

2

Underline the pair of words most similar in meaning. 3

Example	laugh, cry	dog, cat	<u>say, speak</u>
3 it, them	alter, hot	pond, lake	
4 bed, door	cold, icy	try, girl	
5 leaf, worm	fire, house	neat, tidy	
6 drum, baby	story, tale	book, tree	
7 little, small	big, tiny	green, bread	

5

Rearrange the muddled letters so that the sentences make sense. 18

Example My UMM *mum* drinks ETA *tea*.

8 We AST __________ in the back of the ARC __________.

9 The KAO __________ tree was very GIB __________.

10 ADD __________ put on his PAC __________.

3

Change the first word of the third pair in the same way as the other pairs. 27

Example DIG → DOG
FIG → FOG
BIG → *BOG*

11 RAT →	RUT	12 WAN →	WIN	13 MAN →	MEN
CAT →	CUT	BAN →	BIN	PAN →	PEN
BAT →	______	FAN →	______	TAN →	______

14 DOG →	DUG	15 FIT →	FAT
LOG →	LUG	HIT →	HAT
TOG →	______	SIT →	______

5

Underline one word from the brackets so that the sentences make sense. 33

Example The (car, <u>cow</u>, table) was eating grass.

16 The (nurse, table, chair) was writing a letter.

17 The (horse, doctor, cat) washed his hands.

18 The (pig, boy, belt) put on his shoes.

19 The (snow, sun, wind) was white on the ground.

20 The (baby, cot, girl) was doing her homework.

5

In a code CABLE is written as 9 8 7 6 5 45

Write these words using the same code.

21 ACE ______ 22 CAB ______ 23 ALE ______

3

Six children (A, B, C, D, E, F) were asked which games they like. 47

Children who like football	Children who like cricket
B	D
A	A
C	E

24 Who likes both games? ____

25 Who likes neither game? ____

2

25 TOTAL

Paper 11

Underline the word in the brackets closest in meaning to the word in capitals. 4

Example SAD (happy, unhappy, friendly)

1 SMALL (child, little, pram)

2 SHOUT (shop, talk, yell)

3 GREAT (huge, thin, empty)

4 LAD (girl, man, boy) 5

5 TALE (plan, lesson, story)

Add a letter to the front of the capital letters so that the sentences make sense. 30

Example Grass is GREEN.

6 ____REES grow in forests and in gardens.

7 When it is warm we like to ____WIM in the sea.

8 There are several ____AGES in a book.

9 We sit on ____HAIRS.

10 My new ____HOES are hurting my feet. 5

Fill in the missing letter in each sequence. The alphabet has been written out to help you. 35

A B C D E F G H I J K L M N O P Q R S T U V W X Y Z

Example A is to B as C is to D

11 A is to E as B is to ____

12 B is to G as D is to ____

13 C is to F as F is to ____

14 D is to G as G is to ____

15 E is to G as F is to ____ 5

Please note that some questions have more than one possible answer. Every effort has been made to include all the alternatives here but you may occasionally find one that has not been listed.

Paper 1

1–5
- dog, **cat**, **cow**
- boy, **girl**, **man**, **lad**

6 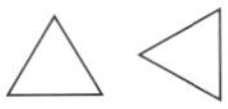

7 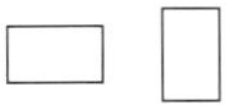

8 IF
9 US
10 BY or ME
11 IS
12 BE
13 seat
14 rice
15 food
16 table
17 sky
18 EBB
19 SEE
20 WEE
21 7
22 7
23 EGG
24 BAD or DAB
25 DEAF or FADE

Paper 2

1 quick, fast
2 boy, lad
3 cat, kitten
4 dog, puppy
5 chair, seat
6 

7 

8 PIT
9 BUT
10 WET
11 NOT
12 BAT
13 CAP HAT PAT
14 BIN PIN TIN
15 JET LET MET
16 BED FED WED
17 ACC
18 CXX
19 RPP
20 16p
21 24p
22 10p
23 20p
24 5
25 3

Paper 3

1 boot
2 mug
3 hurry
4 fresh
5 circle
6 

7 

8 L
9 H
10 H
11 B
12 W
13 E
14 E
15 H
16 E
17 J
18 DAY SAY WAY
19 BIT HIT SIT
20 GET SET WET
21 BOY JOY TOY
22 15p
23 27p
24 10.00
25 15.00

Paper 4

1–3
- **no corners**: b)
- **corners**: a), c)

4 begin, start
5 big, large
6 rain, drizzle
7 cake, bun
8 damp, wet
9 COT
10 ALL
11 LOW
12 ROD
13 FOG
14 melting
15 box
16 fish
17 coat
18 garage
19 man
20 sad
21 swim
22 house
23 puppy
24 12.08
25 13.03

Paper 5

1–5
- scream, **cry**, **shout**, **yell**
- hop, **run**, **walk**

6 IS
7 IN
8 BE
9 MY
10 ME
11 

12 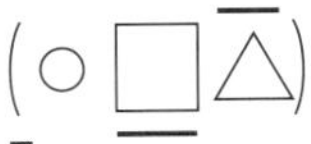

13 7
14 10
15–16 1 3
17 177
18 435
19 576
20 7
21 6
22 8
23 Tuesday
24 Friday
25 Monday

Paper 6

1 cot, bed
2 mug, cup

3 pen, pencil
4 start, begin
5 cry, shout
6

7
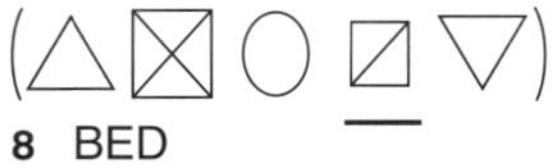
8 BED
9 COT
10 DOG
11 and
12 all
13 TUB
14 MAT
15 POT
16 LAG
17 TAP
18 AD
19 CF
20 DG
21 EH
22 ART
23 TOP
24 NAP
25 EGG

Paper 7

1 tall
2 colour
3 cuddle
4 two
5 see
6 man dog
7 was wet
8 dad tea
9 T
10 T
11 N
12 E
13 E
14 lady
15 bus
16 driver
17 boy
18 girl
19 G
20 G
21 F
22 H
23 H
24

25

Paper 8

1

2

3 close, near
4 small, short
5 jump, hop
6 brush, sweep
7 end, finish
8 nip, pin
9 ink, kin
10 gas, sag
11 HOP
12 MAT
13 OUT
14 ICE
15 OLD
16 4
17 food
18 animal
19 light
20 brush
21 CUP MUG SUP
22 BOG FIG LOG
23 HEN MEN PEN
24 10.00
25 10.30

Paper 9

1–5

6

7

8 CAT
9 COW
10 POT
11 US
12 IF
13 BE
14 AS
15 MY or BE
16 CAN MAN PAN
17 BED LED RED
18 CUT HUT POT
19 ANT BEE EVE
20 ATE BUN SEA
21 214
22 254
23 144
24 Friday 23 December
25 September 9th

Paper 10

1–2 **Fewer than 4 corners** **More than 4 corners**
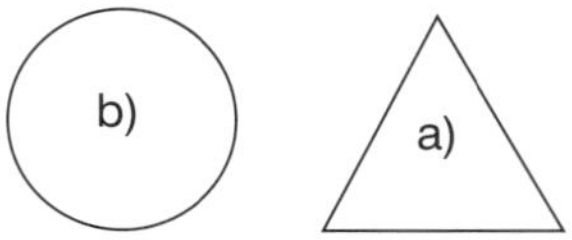

3 pond, lake
4 cold, icy
5 neat, tidy
6 story, tale
7 little, small
8 sat car
9 oak big
10 Dad cap
11 BUT
12 FIN
13 TEN
14 TUG
15 SAT
16 nurse
17 doctor
18 boy
19 snow
20 girl
21 895
22 987
23 865
24 A
25 F

Paper 11

1 little
2 yell
3 huge
4 boy
5 story
6 T
7 S
8 P
9 C
10 S

11 F
12 I
13 I
14 J
15 H
16 
17 
18 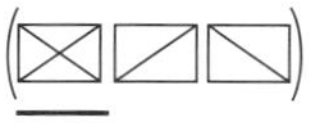
19 8
20 20
21 8
22 18p
23 48p
24 BEAD
25 CAFE

Paper 12

1 
2 
3 dull, dim
4 dish, plate
5 cap, hat
6 near, close
7 shoe, slipper
8 BIN
9 HUT
10 BEE
11 MAN
12 ILL
13 car
14 flower
15 eat
16 ears
17 cake
18 5
19 8
20 11
21 7
22 11.40
23 12.45
24 3
25 40p

Paper 13

1–5 

6 MAT
7 CAT
8 SET
9 BUN
10 DAG or WIG
11 oak
12 cold
13 desk
14 grew
15 girl
16 
17 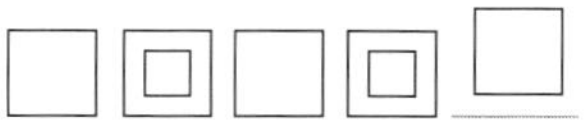
18 
19 187
20 751
21 385
22 10 miles
23 9 miles
24 11
25 8

Paper 14

1 shout, scream
2 cry, sob
3 speak, talk
4 wash, clean
5 plate, dish
6 
7 
8 SET
9 PUP
10 SON
11 JOY
12 RAT
13 FUR MAT RUG
14 BUS CAR ODD
15 DOT HUM PUT
16 OUT SIT TEA
17 gog
18 eng
19 eog
20 90p
21 30p
22 12.02
23 4.30
24 June 3rd
25 Monday

Paper 15

1 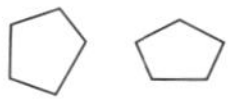
2 
3 
4 slumber
5 begin
6 pick
7 large
8 sob
9 S
10 S
11 A
12 W
13 R
14 R
15 M
16 O
17 S
18 Q
19 CAT DOG PIG
20 COW EAT RED
21 HAT JAR TIE
22 BUT CAR JAM
23 11
24 9
25 9

Paper 16

1–2

Shapes with 1 line	Shapes with more than 1 line
a)	b)

3 wash, clean
4 fit, well

5 lid, top
6 neat, tidy
7 fire, flames
8 sea
9 arm
10 car
11 EAR
12 LAD
13 CAP
14 BAD
15 OWL
16 cot
17 barked
18 zoo
19 shining
20 bone
21 water
22 duck
23 onion
24 fish
25 yellow

Paper 17

1–5 **Food** **Transport**

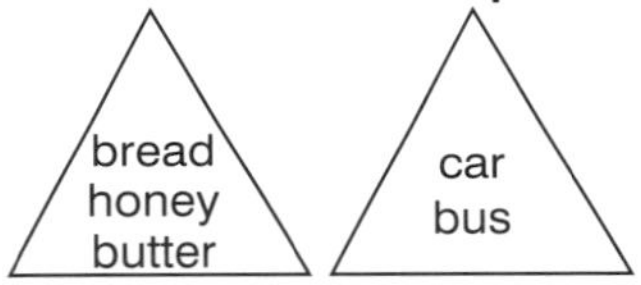

6 not, ton
7 nib, bin
8 pit, tip
9 COP or CAT
10 ODD
11 DRY
12 MAD or SUD
13 PAN
14
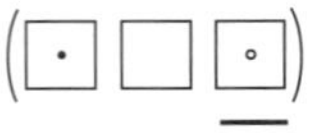

15

16 ABCD
17 BCDE
18 CDEF
19 DEFG
20 GHIJ
21 bce
22 cdb
23 adb
24 13 − **2** = 11
25 7 + **4** = 11

Paper 18

1 tired, sleepy
2 big, huge
3 hurry, rush
4 paint, colour
5 see, look
6

7

8 CUT
9 MUG
10 HAT
11 TOG
12 JET
13 PIN
14 POT
15 RUG
16 2345
17 3456
18 6789
19 5678
20 4567
21 cde
22 ecd
23 bce
24 20p
25 15p

Paper 19

1 pile
2 noisy
3 gap
4 happy
5 lots
6 cat top
7 sun day
8 ate bun
9 P
10 W
11 C
12 S
13 D
14 oranges
15 glass
16 book
17 sandwich
18 song
19 W
20 Z
21 T
22 S
23 P
24
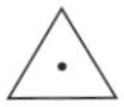

25

Paper 20

1
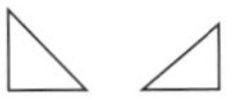

2

3 cup, mug
4 lean, slim
5 halt, stop
6 fast, rapid
7 smash, break
8 pat, tap
9 bad, dab
10 ant, tan
11 ARM
12 CAT
13 HUG
14 BAG
15 BIT
16 beach
17 pedalled
18 ice-cream
19 low
20 doctor
21 HOP ICE JOY
22 NIL ONE TEN
23 ASS PIN WET
24 Town D
25 6°C

Underline one shape in the brackets to complete the sequence. 19

16

17
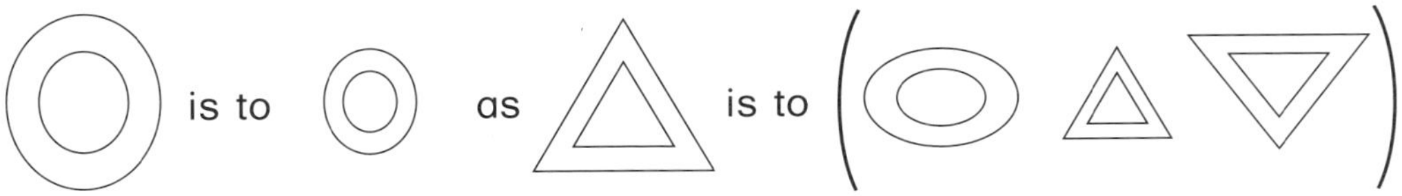

18
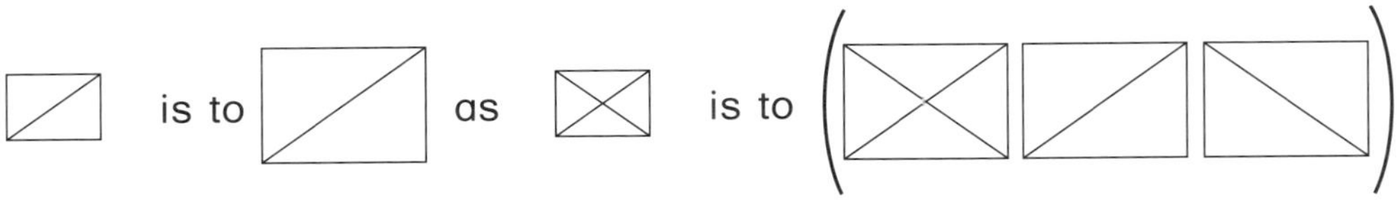

3

Write the missing number in each sequence. 42

Example	1	2	3	4	5
19 10	____	6	4	2	
20 0	10	____	30	40	
21 2	4	6	____	10	

3

A has 10p, B has twice as much as A. C has 2p less than B. 47

22 C has __________. **23** Together they have __________. 2

A B C D E F G H I J K L M N O P Q R S T U V W X Y Z

24 What word is made from the 2nd, 5th, 1st and 4th letters?

____

25 What word is made from the 3rd, 1st, 6th and 5th letters?

____

2

25 TOTAL

Paper 12

Underline the shape in the brackets most similar to the shape outside the brackets.

1 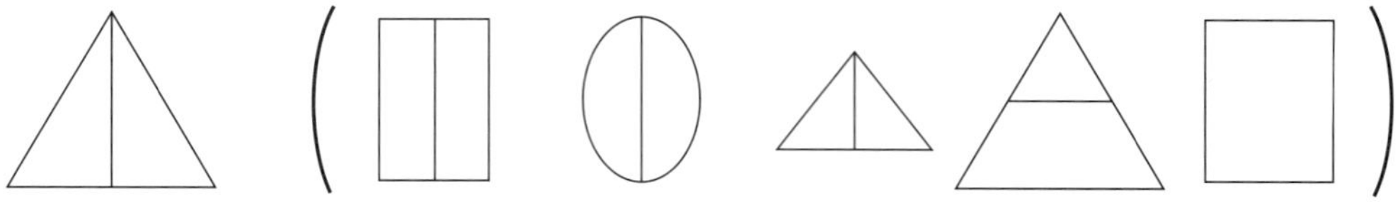

2 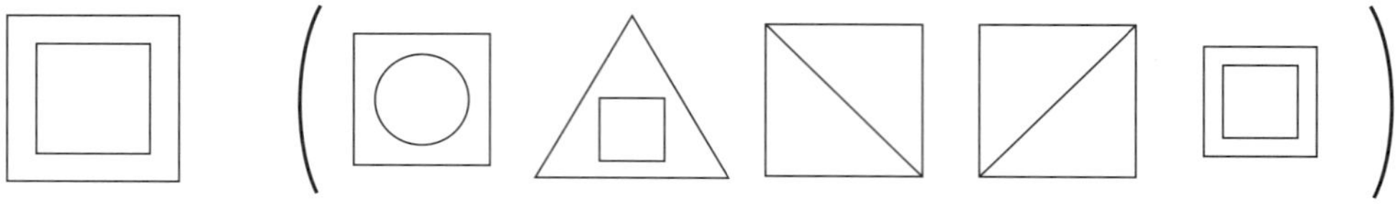

2

Underline the two words, one from each group, which are closest in meaning. 5

Example (shut, open) (close, window)

3 (dull, sky) (bright, dim)

4 (eat, dish) (plate, food)

5 (head, cap) (tall, hat)

6 (near, from) (far, close)

7 (walk, shoe) (slipper, hurry)

5

Remove one letter from the word in capital letters to leave a new word. The meaning of the new word is given in the clue. 31

Example OPEN something you write with PEN

8 BIND we put rubbish in it ______

9 HURT a type of shed ______

10 BEEF an insect ______

11 MEAN a grown-up boy ______

12 MILL not well ______

5

Complete the following expressions by underlining the correct word in the brackets. 37

Example Boy is to girl as man is to (<u>woman</u>, grown-up, person).

13 Hay is to horse as petrol is to (donkey, car, basket).

14 Leaf is to tree as petal is to (forest, flower, cactus).

15 Tired is to sleep as hungry is to (light, eat, sad).

16 Sight is to eyes as sound is to (picture, noise, ears).

17 Cheese is to pizza as icing is to (tomatoes, cake, food). 5

Write the missing number or numbers in each sequence. 42

Example	1	2	3	4	5
18	3	____	7	9	11
19	12	10	____	6	4
20–21	15	13	____	9	____

4

X's watch is 5 minutes slow. 47

22 At 11.45 X's watch will show __________ .

23 At 12.50 it will show __________ . 2

Ten sweets are shared between 3 girls. A has 5 sweets, B has 2 sweets.

24 How many sweets does C have? Underline the correct answer.

2 3 4 5 6

Mum gives B and C £1 between them. She gives B 60p.

25 How much does she give C? Underline the correct answer.

20p 30p 40p 50p 2

25 TOTAL

Paper 13

1–5 Write these words in the correct group. 2

rose star poppy sun tulip

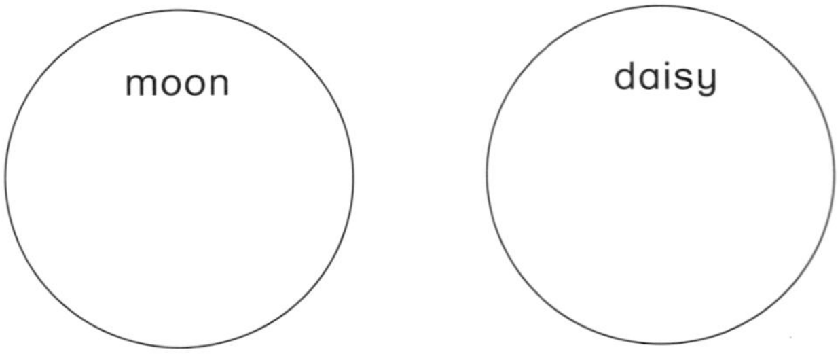

5

Change the first word into the last word by changing one letter at a time. The word in the middle must be a real word. 26

Example ON → AN → AT

6 MAD __________ MET

7 CAN __________ CUT

8 SAT __________ WET

9 BUT __________ SUN

10 DIG __________ WAG 5

33

Underline one word from the brackets so that the sentences make sense.

Example The (car, <u>cow</u>, table) was eating grass.

11 The (rose, oak, daisy) is a big tree.

12 She put on her gloves as she was (hot, wet, cold).

13 The (desk, pot, shoe) was full of books.

14 The rose (sat, grew, cried) in the garden.

15 The (horse, girl, sailor) walked to school. 5

Draw the missing shape in each sequence.

16

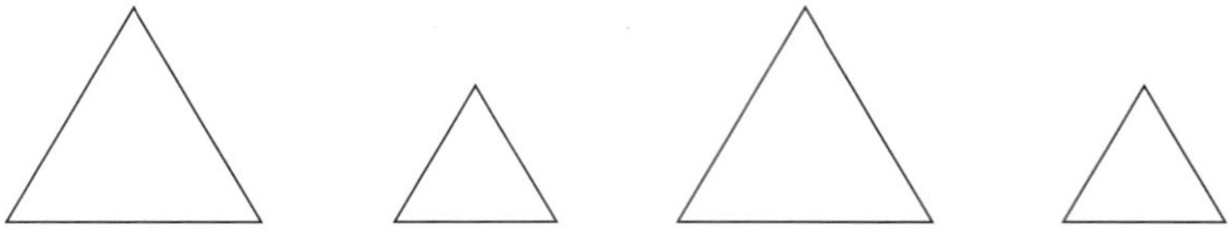 __________

17 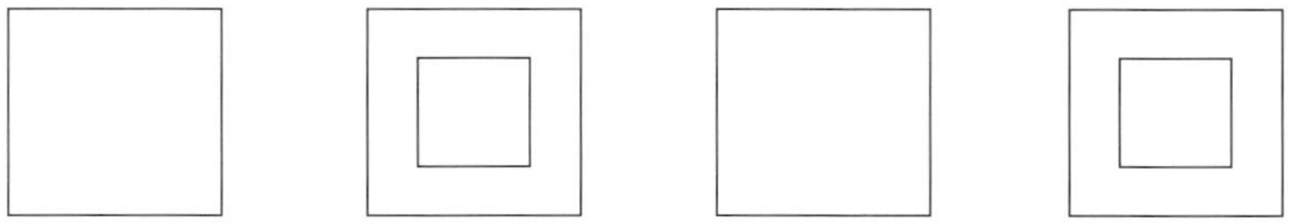 ________

18 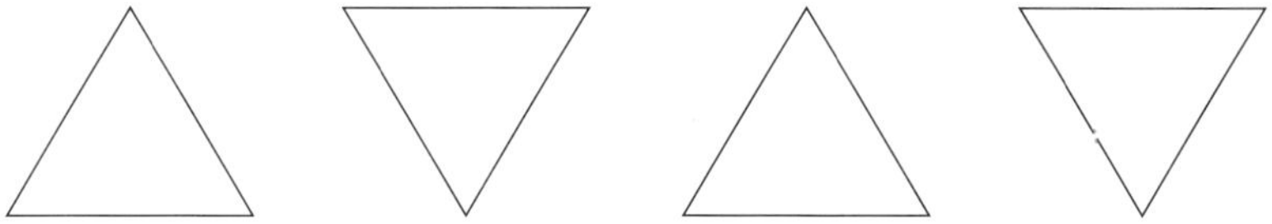 ________ 3

In a code PLANE is written as 1 3 5 7 8 45

Write these words using the same code.

19 PEN ________ 20 NAP ________ 21 LEA ________ 3

In a race A ran 5 miles. B ran twice as far as A, and C ran a mile less than B. 47

22 B ran ________ . 23 C ran ________ . 2

Fill in the missing number in each line.

24	7	8	9	10	____	12
25	2	4	6	____	10	12

2

25 TOTAL

Paper 14

Underline the pair of words most similar in meaning. 3

Example	laugh, cry	dog, cat	say, speak
1	leg, face	hop, run	shout, scream
2	cry, sob	nasty, nice	slow, quick
3	doll, pram	speak, talk	toy, book
4	cold, milk	paper, fish	wash, clean
5	drink, dance	hold, drop	plate, dish

5

Underline the two shapes, one from each group, that are most similar.

6 

7 

2

Change the first word of the third pair in the same way as the other pairs. 27

Example DIG → DOG
FIG → FOG
BIG → *BOG*

8 MAT → MET
PAT → PET
SAT → ____________

9 SOP → SUP
COP → CUP
POP → ____________

10 WIN → WON
TIN → TON
SIN → ____________

11 BAY → BOY
HAY → HOY
JAY → ____________

12 CAN → CAT
POT → PAT
ROT → ____________

5

Write these words in alphabetical order. 43

Example TRUCK CAR BUS VAN *BUS CAR TRUCK VAN*

13 MAT FUR RUG

(1) ____________ (2) ____________ (3) ____________

14 CAR BUS ODD

(1) ____________ (2) ____________ (3) ____________

15 DOT PUT HUM

(1) ____________ (2) ____________ (3) ____________

16 SIT TEA OUT

(1) ____________ (2) ____________ (3) ____________ 4

In a code DIAL is written as g o n e 45

Write these words using the same code.

17 DID ____________ 18 LAD ____________ 19 LID ____________ 3

X has 20p. Y has twice as much as X and Z has 10p less than Y. 47

20 Together they have ____________. 21 Z has ____________. 2

Underline the earliest of these times.

22 12.10 12.05 12.02 12.20

Underline the latest of these times.

23 4.02 4.30 4.03 4.25 2

24 June 1st is a Tuesday. What will be the date on the Thursday of that week?

____

25 What day of the week was the last day in May? ____________ 2

25 TOTAL

Paper 15

Underline the pair of shapes that are most similar.

1

2

3  3

Underline the word in the brackets closest in meaning to the word in capitals. 4

Example SAD (happy, <u>unhappy</u>, friendly)

4 SLEEP (bed, slumber, cot)

5 START (win, lose, begin)

6 CHOOSE (best, pick, win)

7 BIG (small, tiny, large)

8 CRY (laugh, dry, sob) 5

Add a letter to the front of the capital letters so that the sentences make sense. 30

Example Grass is GREEN.

9–13 There are 4 seasons: ____PRING, ____UMMER, ____UTUMN

and ____INTER.

It is wet when it ____AINS. 5

Fill in the missing letter in each sequence. The alphabet has been written out to help you. 35

A B C D E F G H I J K L M N O P Q R S T U V W X Y Z

Example A is to B as C is to D

14 M is to P as O is to ____

15 J is to L as K is to ____

16 L is to N as M is to ____

17 P is to Q as R is to ____

18 P is to R as O is to ____ 5

Write these words in alphabetical order. 43

Example TRUCK CAR BUS VAN *BUS CAR TRUCK VAN*

19 DOG CAT PIG

(1) ________ (2) ________ (3) ________

20 COW RED EAT

(1) ________ (2) ________ (3) ________

21 TIE HAT JAR

(1) ________ (2) ________ (3) ________

22 BUT JAM CAR

(1) ________ (2) ________ (3) ________ 4

If a = 1 b = 2 c = 3 d = 4 e = 5 what is the value of the following? 49

23 b + e + d = ________

24 e + b + b = ________

25 a + c + e = ________ 3

25 TOTAL

Paper 16

1–2 Write the letter of each shape in the correct group.

a)

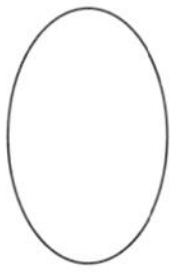

b)

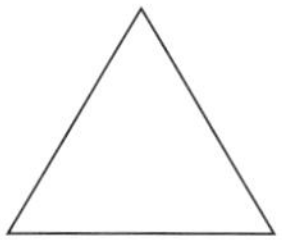

Shapes with 1 line	**Shapes with more than 1 line**

2

Underline the two words, one from each group, which are closest in meaning. 5

Example (shut, open) (close, window)

3 (wash, water) (soap, clean)

4 (ill, fit) (well, doctor)

5 (bottle, lid) (top, bottom)

6 (neat, work) (mess, tidy)

7 (fire, rest) (work, flames) 5

Underline the one word in each group which cannot be made from the letters in capitals. 19

Example ABCD bad cad ace dab

8 MARKS ark mar ram sea

9 STEAM mat arm sea tea

10 COAST cat cot car sat 3

Remove one letter from the word in capital letters to leave a new word. The meaning of the new word is given in the clue. 31

Example OPEN something you write with PEN

11 BEAR we hear with this ___________

12 LEAD a boy ___________

13 CARP we put it on our head ___________

14 BAND not good ___________

15 BOWL a bird which hoots ___________ 5

Underline one word from the brackets so that the sentences make sense. 33

Example The (car, cow, table) was eating grass.

16 Mum put the baby in her (box, cot, shed).

17 The dog (sang, cried, barked).

18 The lion was in the (shop, sea, zoo).

19 The moon was (shining, singing, dancing).

20 He gave the dog a (bus, board, bone). 5

Complete the following expressions by underlining the correct word in the brackets. 37

Example Boy is to girl as man is to (<u>woman</u>, grown-up, person).

21 Bird is to sky as fish is to (sand, earth, water).

22 Chick is to chicken as duckling is to (dog, goose, duck).

23 Salt is to vinegar as cheese is to (pepper, onion, fish).

24 Fur is to rabbit as scales are to (fish, bird, hair).

25 Tomato is to red as banana is to (blue, purple, yellow). 5

25 TOTAL

Paper 17

1–5 Write these words in the correct group. 2

bread car bus honey butter

Food

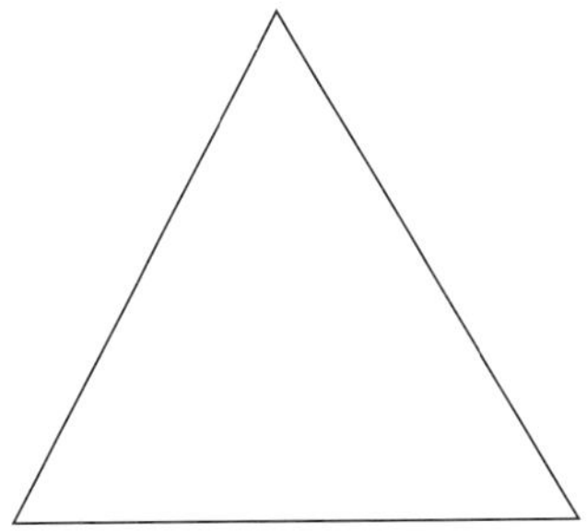

Transport

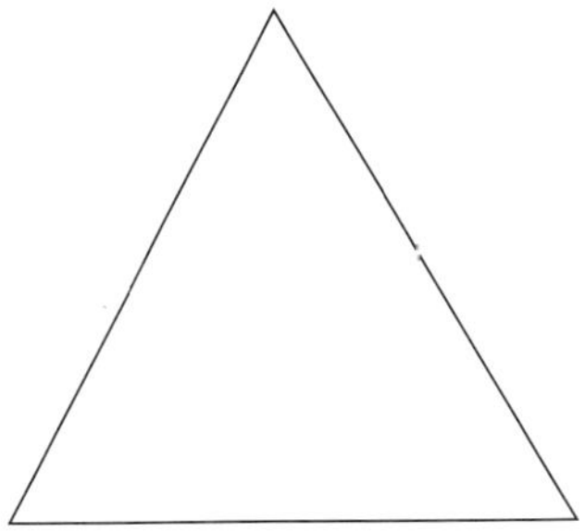

5

Underline the two words which are made from the same letters. 22

Example <u>two</u> too <u>tow</u> wet ten

6 not nut ten ton tan

7 tab tub nib nab bin

8 pit top put tip pat 3

Change the first word into the last word by changing one letter at a time. The word in the middle must be a real word. 26

Example ON → AN → AT

9 COT ________ CAP

10 OLD ________ ADD

11 CRY ________ DAY

12 SAD ________ MUD

13 PIN ________ CAN 5

Underline one shape in the brackets to complete the sequence.

14

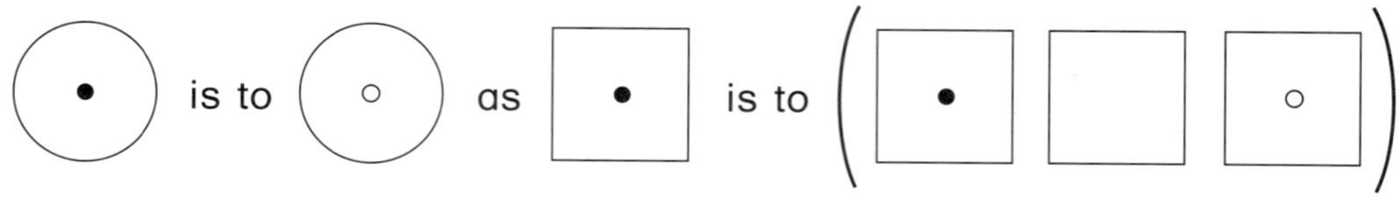

15

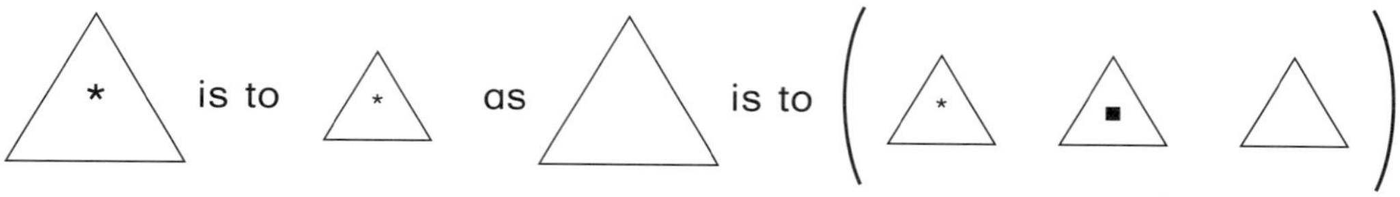

2

Give the next group of letters in each sequence. 41

Example A B C D

16 A AB ABC ________

17 B BC BCD ________

18 C CD CDE ________

19 D DE DEF ________

20 G GH GHI ________ 5

In a code BREAD is written as a b c d e 45

Write these words using the same code.

21 RED ________ 22 EAR ________ 23 BAR ________ 3

Fill in the missing figures. 50

24 13 – _____ = 11 **25** 7 + _____ = 11 2

25 TOTAL

Paper 18

Underline the pair of words most similar in meaning.

Example laugh, cry dog, cat <u>say, speak</u> 3

1	cry, laugh	give, game	tired, sleepy
2	under, out	big, huge	rain, small
3	short, long	heavy, light	hurry, rush
4	paint, colour	hot, meal	far, near
5	run, fall	bad, good	see, look

5

Underline the shape in the brackets most similar to the first shape.

6

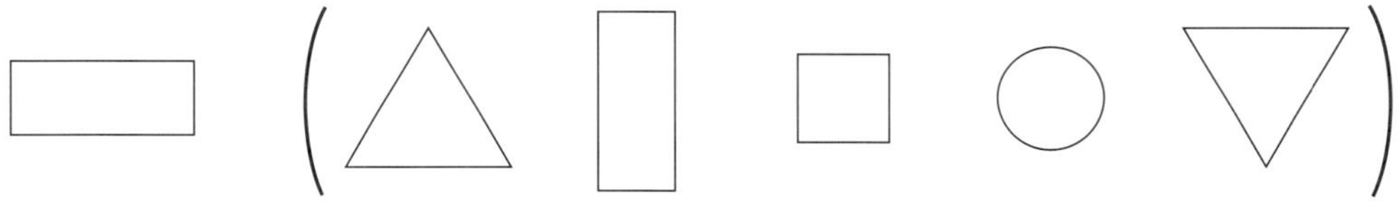

7

2

Rearrange the muddled letters to make a proper word so that the sentences make sense. 17

Example I can read a KOBO. BOOK

8 Dad UCT the grass. _______________

9 She had her drink in a UGM. _______________

10 He put a THA on his head. _______________

3

Change the first word of the third pair in the same way as the other pairs. 27

Example DIG → DOG
FIG → FOG
BIG → BOG

11 FAG → FOG
LAG → LOG
TAG → ______

12 NUT → NET
BUT → BET
JUT → ______

13 SUN → SIN
BUN → BIN
PUN → ______

14 CAT → COT
HAT → HOT
PAT → ______

15 FIG → FUG
BIG → BUG
RIG → ______

5

Write the missing number in each sequence. 42

Example 1 2 3 4 5

16	2	23	234	______
17	3	34	345	______
18	6	67	678	______
19	5	56	567	______
20	4	45	456	______

5

In a code PLEAT is written as a b c d e 45

Write these words using the same code.

21 EAT ______ **22** TEA ______ **23** LET ______

3

Underline the correct answer each time. 50

I have 35p. If I spend 15p how much will I have left?

24 15p 16p 18p 20p

I have 20p. If I spend 5p how much will I have left?

25 10p 12p 15p 16p

2

25 TOTAL

Paper 19

Underline the word in the brackets closest in meaning to the word in capitals. 4

Example SAD (happy, <u>unhappy</u>, friendly)

1 HEAP (stones, pile, heal)

2 LOUD (quiet, soft, noisy)

3 HOLE (mend, gap, dig)

4 GLAD (happy, sad, sorry)

5 MANY (few, lots, little) 5

Rearrange the muddled letters so that the sentences make sense. 18

Example My UMM *mum* drinks ETA *tea*.

6 The ACT __________ sat on OTP __________ of the wall.

7 The NUS __________ shone all YAD __________.

8 The girl TAE __________ a NUB __________. 3

Add a letter to the front of the capital letters so that the sentences make sense. 30

Example Grass is *G*REEN.

9 We go in a ____LANE so we can fly in the sky.

10–11 We ____ASH to keep ourselves ____LEAN.

12 It is cold when it ____NOWS.

13 It is ____ARK at night. 5

Underline one word from the brackets so that the sentences make sense. 33

Example The (car, <u>cow</u>, table) was eating grass.

14 She went to the shop for some (oranges, weeds, holes).

15 The window was made of (bricks, glass, tiles).

16 The boy read the (button, cloth, book).

17 He ate his (sandwich, satchel, story).

18 She sang a (dance, lesson, song). 5

Fill in the missing letter in each sequence. The alphabet has been written out to help you. 35

A B C D E F G H I J K L M N O P Q R S T U V W X Y Z

Example A is to B as C is to D

19 S is to T as V is to ____

20 S is to V as W is to ____

21 P is to S as Q is to ____

22 O is to R as P is to ____

23 K is to N as M is to ____ 5

Draw the missing shape in each sequence.

24

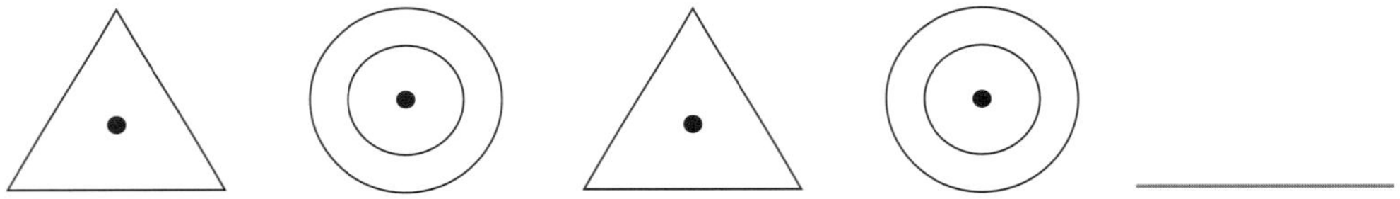

25

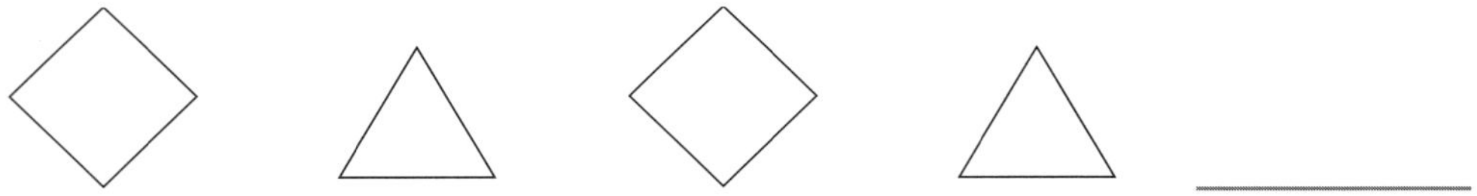

2

25 TOTAL

Paper 20

Underline the pair of shapes that are most similar.

1

2  2

Underline the two words, one from each group, which are closest in meaning. 5

Example (shut, open) (close, window)

3 (drink, cup) (plate, mug)

4 (lean, fat) (foot, slim)

5 (halt, red) (stop, travel)

6 (food, fast) (slow, rapid)

7 (smash, toy) (mend, break) 5

Underline the two words which are made from the same letters. 22

Example two, too, tow, wet, ten

8 put pat top pet tap

9 bid bud bad dab bed

10 ant ton ten tin tan 3

Remove one letter from the word in capital letters to leave a new word. The meaning of the new word is given in the clue. 31

Example OPEN something you write with PEN

11 HARM part of your body ____________

12 CANT an animal that mews ____________

13 HUGE to have a cuddle ____________

14 BRAG we put our shopping in this ____________

15 BITE a small piece ____________ 5

Complete the following expressions by underlining the correct word in the brackets. 37

Example Boy is to girl as man is to (<u>woman</u>, grown-up, person).

16 Grass is to lawn as sand is to (beach, sea, hills).

17 Car is to driven as bike is to (pedalled, crawled, cried).

18 Hot is to pie as cold is to (coat, ice-cream, blanket).

19 Mountain is to high as valley is to (fast, slow, low).

20 Garage is to mechanic as hospital is to (car, doctor, plumber). 5

Write these words in alphabetical order. 43

Example TRUCK CAR BUS VAN BUS CAR TRUCK VAN

21 HOP JOY ICE

(1) ________ (2) ________ (3) ________

22 TEN ONE NIL

(1) ________ (2) ________ (3) ________

23 WET PIN ASS

(1) ________ (2) ________ (3) ________ 3

These were the temperatures in some towns last Monday. 47

Town A 5°C	Town B 7°C	Town C 10°C	Town D 4°C	Town E 6°C

24 Which town had the lowest temperature? ________

25 How much colder was it than Town C? ________ 2

25 TOTAL

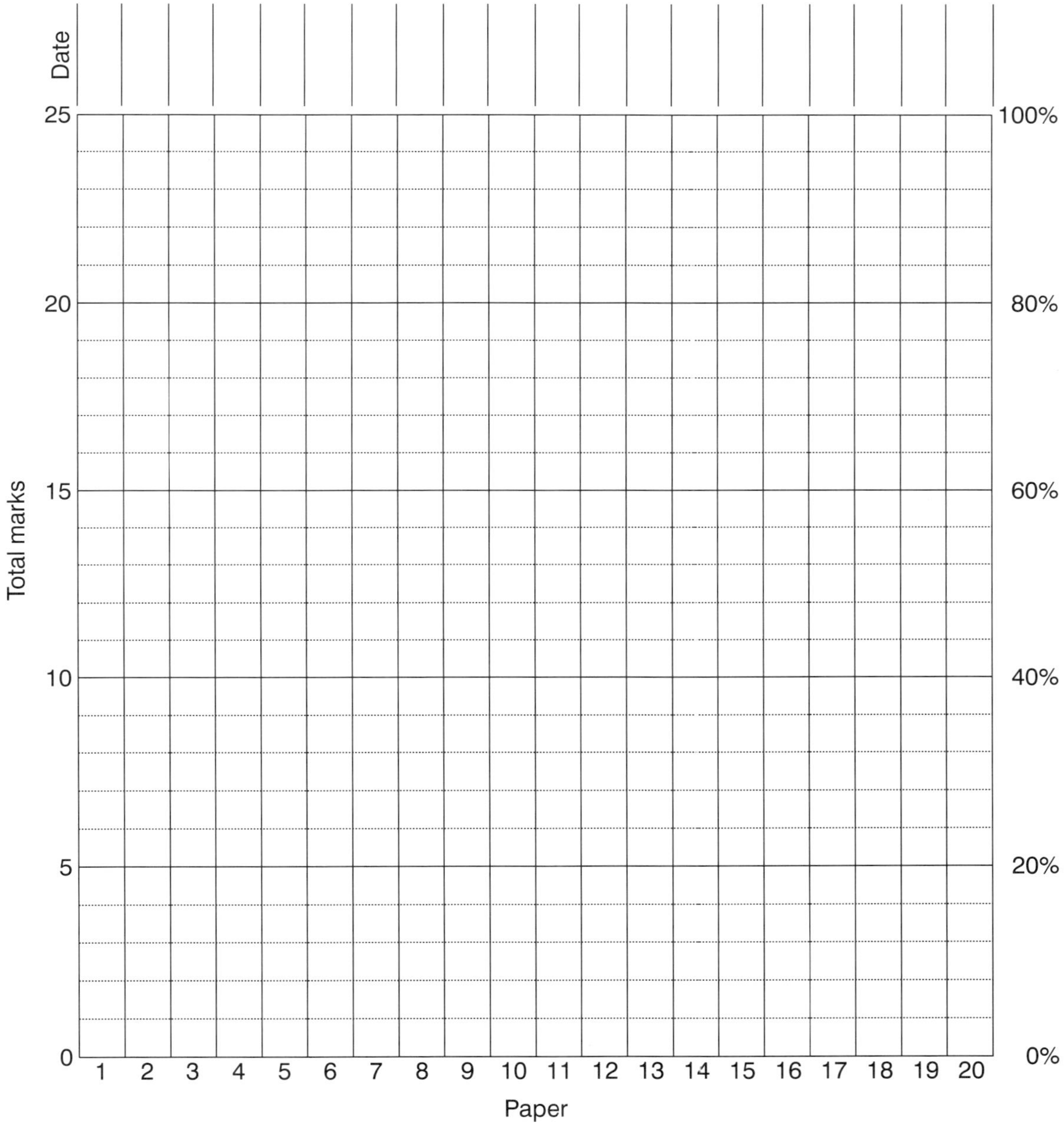
Date
Total marks
25
20
15
10
5
0
100%
80%
60%
40%
20%
0%
1 2 3 4 5 6 7 8 9 10 11 12 13 14 15 16 17 18 19 20
Paper